· CHARLIE WATSON ·

Explorers

Atlas in the Round

RUNNING PRESS

PHILADELPHIA · LONDON

Contents

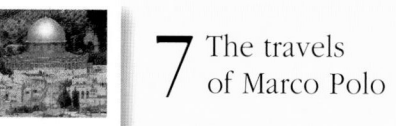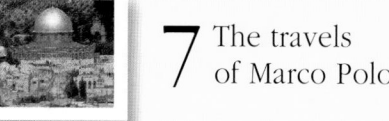

 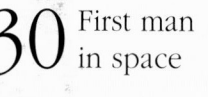
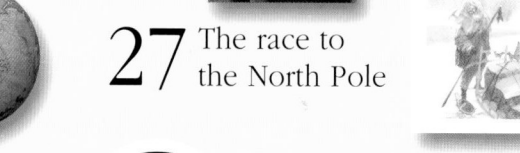
9 8 7 6 5 4 3 2

Digit on the right indicates the number of this printing

Library of Congress Cataloging-in-publication number 2001087028

ISBN 0-7624-1036-1

Copyright © 2001 The Ilex Press Ltd
Devised and produced by The Ilex Press Ltd,
1 West End, Whittlesford, Cambridge CB2 4LX, UK

All rights reserved under the Pan-American and International Copyright Conventions.

Color separations: DPI
Printed in China

Art Director: Alastair Campbell
Managing Editor: Kim Yarwood
Project Manager: Elizabeth Wyse
Production Editor: Jannie Brightman
Design Manager: Kevin McGeoghegan
Designer: Michael Leaman
Cover design: Stephen Minns
Maps: Nicholas Rowland, Digital Wisdom Publishing Ltd.

This book may be ordered by mail from the publisher. Please include $2.50 for postage and handling. *But try your bookstore first!*

Running Press Book Publishers
125 South Twenty-Second Street
Philadelphia, Pennsylvania 19103-4399

visit us on the web!
www.runningpress.com

Introduction

Imagine you are an explorer. As you step into the unknown, you have no way of knowing when, or if, you will return home. Are your supplies and equipment good enough? Will you be attacked by hostile people or wild animals? Will you and your fellow pioneers survive the extreme temperatures or howling, mid-ocean storms? It is impossible to say. The only thing you know for sure is that it will be one of the toughest experiences of your life. In the *Atlas of Explorers* you will travel with the world's greatest explorers, as they cross oceans, deserts, and jungles, to discover new continents and new civilizations, or simply to go where no human being has ever gone before. Venture into Mongolia with Marco Polo. Cross the Atlantic with Viking Leif Eriksson. Discover Australia with Captain Cook, and visit the moon with Neil Armstrong and Buzz Aldrin.

As you share in the discoveries of these and many other great travelers, you will also find out why they made their perilous journeys. Some

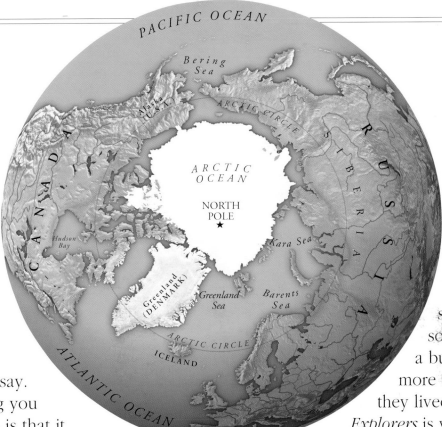

Above *Edmund Hillary and Tenzing Norgay, the climbers who conquered Mt. Everest.*

sought gold or land, some wanted fame, and some were driven by a burning need to know more about the world they lived in. The *Atlas of Explorers* is your opportunity to relive some of the most incredible journeys ever made.

Right *Yuri Gagarin, the Russian cosmonaut*

Above *Christopher Columbus meeting the natives of the Caribbean islands.*

Above *Vasco da Gama's ship*

Key to the maps
Mapmakers use symbols to give information. The symbols shown here form a Key to the information given in this ATLAS IN THE ROUND. For example, three symbols are used for cities. Can you see the difference between them?

- ⬤ Capital cities
- ● Cities
- ⸭ Ancient sites
- ✕ Battles
- ∼ Rivers
- ∼ International borders
- ∼ State/Territory borders
- ▲ Mountain peaks

Great general and explorer

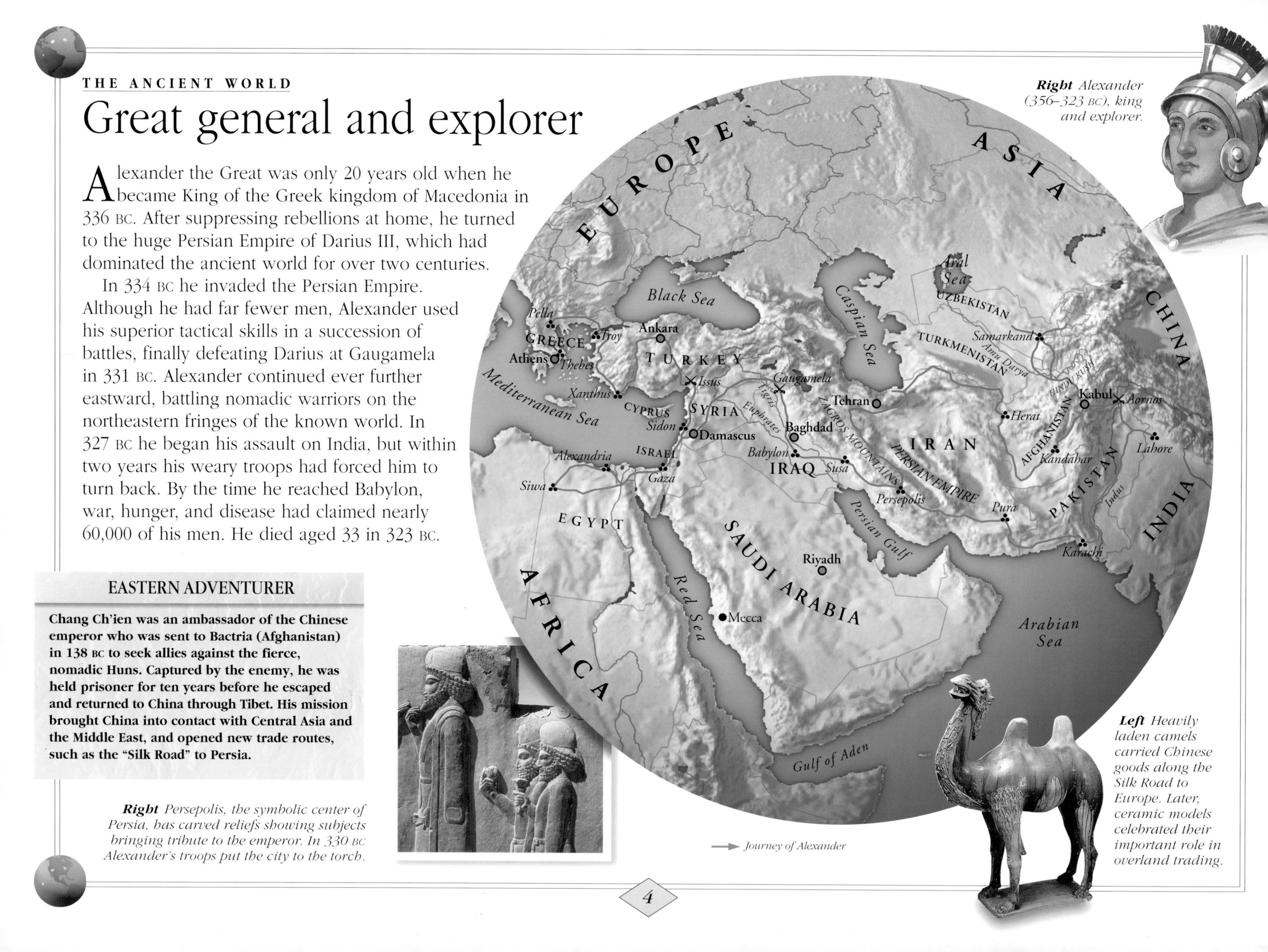

Right *Alexander (356–323 BC), king and explorer.*

Alexander the Great was only 20 years old when he became King of the Greek kingdom of Macedonia in 336 BC. After suppressing rebellions at home, he turned to the huge Persian Empire of Darius III, which had dominated the ancient world for over two centuries.

In 334 BC he invaded the Persian Empire. Although he had far fewer men, Alexander used his superior tactical skills in a succession of battles, finally defeating Darius at Gaugamela in 331 BC. Alexander continued ever further eastward, battling nomadic warriors on the northeastern fringes of the known world. In 327 BC he began his assault on India, but within two years his weary troops had forced him to turn back. By the time he reached Babylon, war, hunger, and disease had claimed nearly 60,000 of his men. He died aged 33 in 323 BC.

EASTERN ADVENTURER

Chang Ch'ien was an ambassador of the Chinese emperor who was sent to Bactria (Afghanistan) in 138 BC to seek allies against the fierce, nomadic Huns. Captured by the enemy, he was held prisoner for ten years before he escaped and returned to China through Tibet. His mission brought China into contact with Central Asia and the Middle East, and opened new trade routes, such as the "Silk Road" to Persia.

Right *Persepolis, the symbolic center of Persia, has carved reliefs showing subjects bringing tribute to the emperor. In 330 BC Alexander's troops put the city to the torch.*

→ *Journey of Alexander*

Left *Heavily laden camels carried Chinese goods along the Silk Road to Europe. Later, ceramic models celebrated their important role in overland trading.*

Pioneering seafarer

Around 300 BC, the geographer Pytheas of Massalia (modern-day Marseilles) was the first Greek to visit the British Isles and Europe's Atlantic coast. His account of his voyages has been lost, but is referred to by later writers.

Pytheas was curious to find the reputed source of tin. He eventually reached Cornwall and visited the tin mines there as well as an island called Ictis (probably St. Michael's Mount). He sailed on along the west coast of Britain and accurately estimated the length of its coastline at 4,000 miles (6,437 km). Sailing across the North Sea, possibly as far as the Baltic, he discovered a source of amber, in the Elbe estuary, or Denmark.

→ Route of Pytheas

⋯ Conjectural route

Above The island Pytheas called "Thule" was six days' journey from Scotland.

This land of the midnight sun was probably Iceland or one of the Shetland Islands.

Right Ptolemy (c. AD 90–168) astronomer and geographer.

Right Ptolemy laid out the geography of the known world by AD 150. His map of classical Eurasia was copied many times in the Middle Ages.

Below Greek ships were powered by oar and sail. Navigational knowledge was very limited. Pytheas was an experienced seafarer, but his journey took him along coasts where he had no knowledge of the prevailing winds. He probably used a lead line to determine the depth of water in shallow areas, and navigated by observing the position of his ship in relation to the sun and the Pole Star.

5

Passage to India

On November 22, 1497, a small Portuguese fleet, commanded by Vasco da Gama, rounded Africa's southern tip in search of a route to the spices of Asia.

Aided by a friendly east African navigator the fleet arrived in Calicut on India's southwestern coast on May 20, 1498. Da Gama insulted Zamorin, the powerful local king, with worthless trinkets and made a hasty departure in August, but had succeeded in opening a trade route to India.

Da Gama finally reached Lisbon in September 1499.

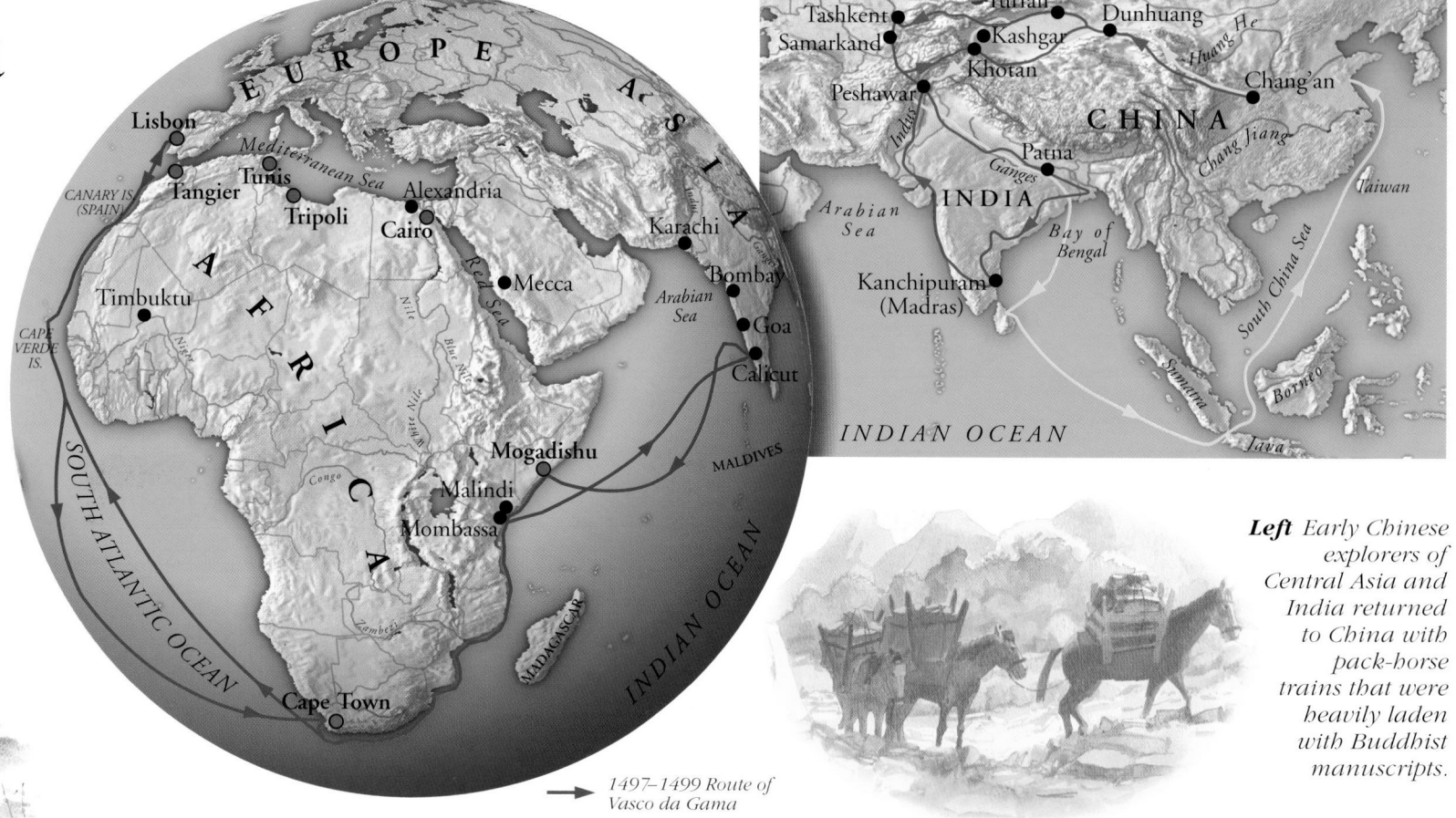

→ *1497–1499 Route of Vasco da Gama*

Left Early Chinese explorers of Central Asia and India returned to China with pack-horse trains that were heavily laden with Buddhist manuscripts.

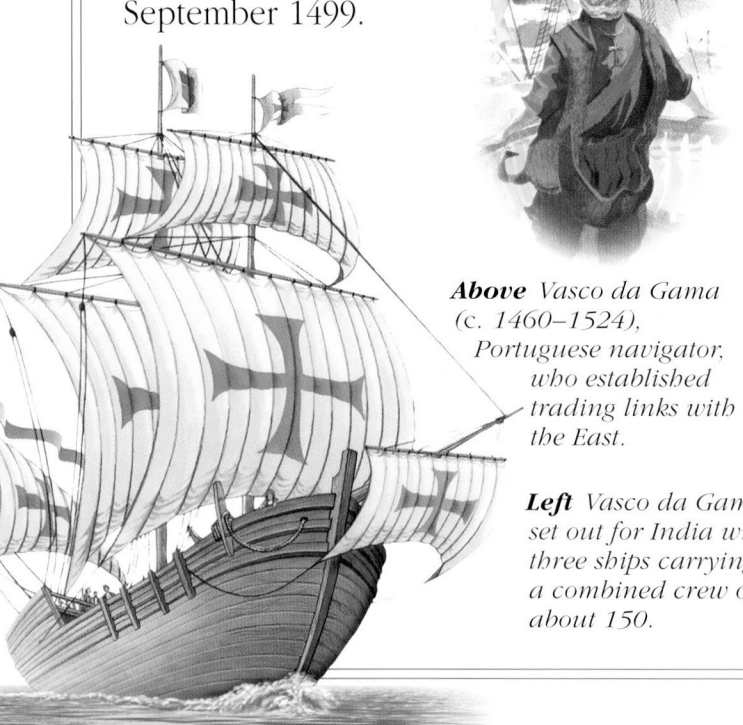

Above *Vasco da Gama (c. 1460–1524), Portuguese navigator, who established trading links with the East.*

Left *Vasco da Gama set out for India with three ships carrying a combined crew of about 150.*

Above *The Cape of Good Hope, the southern tip of Africa, was first rounded in 1488 by Bartholomeu Dias who named it "Cabo Tormentoso" (Cape of Storms).*

IN THE NAME OF GOD

Religion was a powerful motive for early travelers in Asia, whether the travelers were themselves Buddhists, Hindus, Muslims, or Christians. In 399, for instance, the Chinese Buddhist monk Fa Hsien skirted the southern edge of the Takla Makan desert and crossed into India through the snows of the northern Himalayas. In 629 Hsüan Tsang, another pioneering Buddhist, first traveled extensively in central Asia and then followed Fa Hsien's footsteps into India, returning to China in 645 with hundreds of relics, manuscripts, and prayer wheels.

More than a thousand years later, in 1661, two Catholic priests sought an overland route from China to India. Austrian-born Johann Gruebner left Beijing in October with Frenchman Albert d'Orville. They became the first Europeans to visit the forbidden Tibetan city of Lhasa, which no European would do again for another 200 years.

The travels of Marco Polo

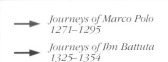

Legend:
- Journeys of Marco Polo 1271–1295
- Journeys of Ibn Battuta 1325–1354
- Ibn Battuta return journey 1346–1349
- .... Ibn Battuta possible journey (to Beijing)

In 1271, the 17-year-old Venetian Marco Polo accompanied his father and uncle to the court of Kublai Khan, the Mongol Emperor of China, at Shang-tu. The Khan was impressed by the young man and accepted his offer of service. Marco stayed for 17 years, acting as the Khan's personal messenger and reporter and receiving a golden safe-conduct pass that required people across the Khan's empire to help him on his way.

The journey home took three years via Sumatra, Sri Lanka, and India.

On his return Marco Polo served briefly in the Venetian fleet in its war with Genoa and was captured and imprisoned. During this time he compiled an account of his journey which was to influence generations of travelers.

Above In 1271, when Niccolo, Maffeo, and Marco Polo arrived at the court of Kublai Khan they brought oil from the lamp of the holy sepulchre in Jerusalem.

Left The Mongols, mounted on stocky ponies, were fine horsemen. They could accurately fire arrows at a fast gallop.

THIRTY YEARS ON THE ROAD

Ibn Battuta was an Islamic scholar who set out from Tangier in 1325 on his first pilgrimage to Mecca. Thirty years later he had traveled over 75,000 miles (120,700 km) through Africa, Europe, and Asia. Traveling as far east as China, where he had been sent as an ambassador by an Indian sultan, Battuta eventually returned home to describe his journeys in a *rihla*, a type of scholarly handbook.

Right Marco Polo (1254–1324), merchant and traveler, spent 17 years in the service of Kublai Khan, the Mongol ruler of China.

A buccaneer's life

The English pirate William Dampier began his first circumnavigation of the globe in 1679. He was involved in a huge privateering expedition with 500 men and nine ships traveling to the Americas and Australia. He made a perilous journey by canoe from the Nicobar Islands to Sumatra, continuing alone to India and Indochina. In 1691, he returned to England.

In 1699, he led a naval expedition to Australia and New Guinea but it was beset by illness and near-mutiny. His third voyage, in 1703, also ended unhappily, limping back to England with the remnants of his crew in 1707. He set sail a year later, capturing the *Encarnacion*, a galley laden with silks, porcelain, and spices.

At the end of a dramatic and often lawless career at sea that included three circumnavigations of the world, Dampier eventually retired to London, where he died in 1715.

Right
William Dampier (c. 1651–1715), English buccaneer and explorer

Right *Dampier discovered a rich tribal culture on his 1699 journey to New Guinea.*

→ *Southeast Asian explorations of William Dampier, 1699*

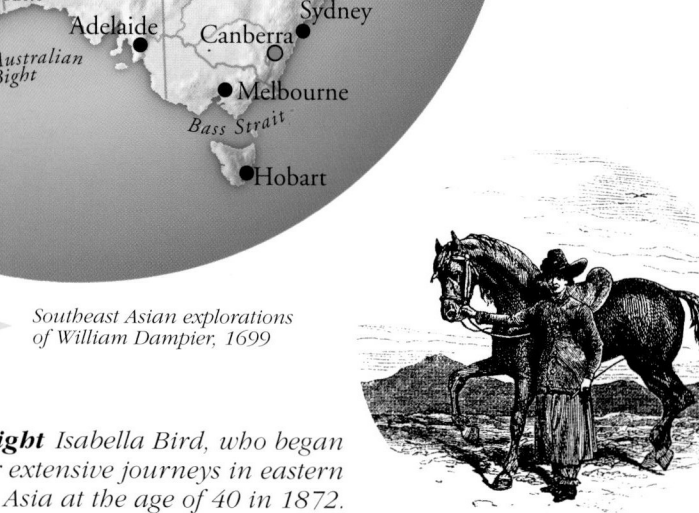

Right *Isabella Bird, who began her extensive journeys in eastern Asia at the age of 40 in 1872.*

A VICTORIAN LADY IN THE EAST

Isabella Bird started traveling in 1872 at the age of 40. Her life as a clergyman's daughter had been stifling and dull and, after years of back trouble, she came to the conclusion that only a complete change would improve her health and her life.

Bird's life was transformed first by a grueling sea voyage and then a prolonged stay in Honolulu. She later visited Japan, traveled in America's Rocky Mountains, and ventured as far as China, Korea, and Tibet.

Right and below *On her trip to the East, Isabella Bird saw much of traditional Japanese culture—such as geisha girls and Shinto temples.*

On top of the world

The Himalayan peak of Mount Everest, at 29,028 feet (8,848 m), is the highest mountain in the world. In the early 1950s, the summit had not yet been reached.

In March, New Zealander Edmund Hillary and the Sherpa, Tenzing Norgay set off from their base camp on the Khumbu Glacier, at 17,572 feet (5,356 m), reaching the Southeast Ridge at the end of May. On May 29, 1953, they struck out for the summit, cutting steps in the snow above an alarming precipice and scaling a 40-foot (12-m) rock wall with crampons and ice axes. By 11:30 a.m., Tenzing and Hillary were standing on the highest spot on earth.

Above *Edmund Hillary and Tenzing Norgay, who climbed Everest in 1953.*

Left *To the Tibetans, Everest is the "goddess mother of the world." To Sherpa tribespeople it is "the mountain so high that no bird can fly over it."*

→ *Journey of Ippolito Desideri 1714–16*

INTO THE UNKNOWN

Jesuit priest Antonio de Andrade was the first European to cross the Himalayas. Disguised as Hindus, he and two Indian Christians set out in 1624 to investigate unconfirmed rumors of Christian communities in Tibet. After joining a Hindu pilgrimage to the shrine at Badrinath, de Andrade entered Tibet. At Tsaparang he founded a mission.

In 1714, meanwhile, the Italian Ippolito Desideri traveled with his Portuguese companion Manuel Freyre from Lahore to Kashmir. After recovering from snow blindness and other ailments, they reached Leh, on the Tibetan plateau, the following year. The pair went on to Lhasa—the home of the Dalai Lama, the leader of Tibetan Buddhism—where Desideri stayed until 1721. Having learned to speak Tibetan, Desideri revisited Tibet several times before he returned to Europe in 1727.

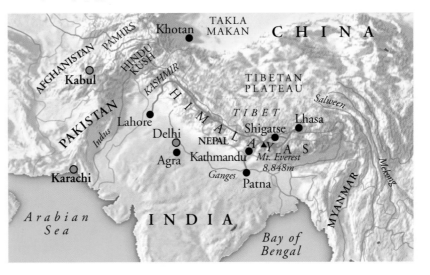

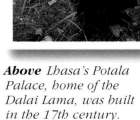

Above *Lhasa's Potala Palace, home of the Dalai Lama, was built in the 17th century.*

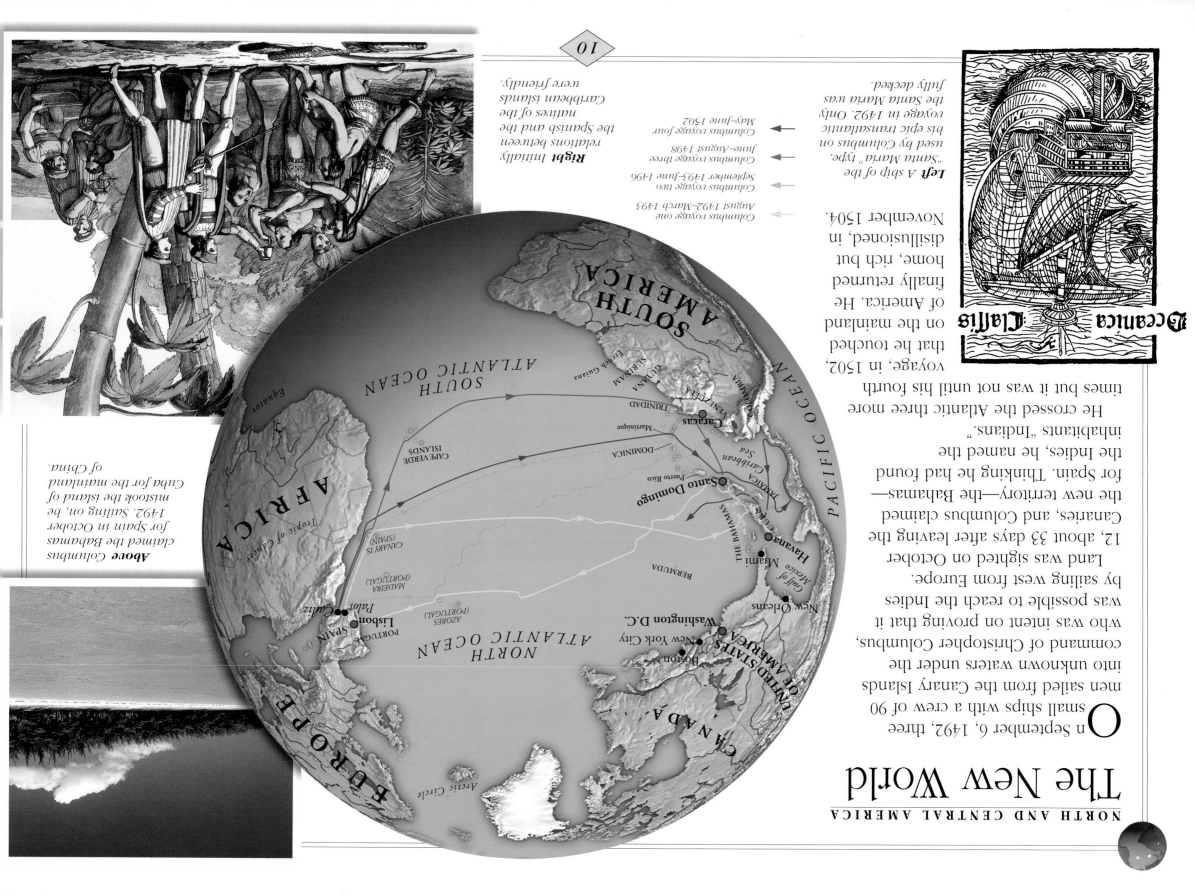

NORTH AND CENTRAL AMERICA

The New World

On September 6, 1492, three small ships with a crew of 90 men sailed from the Canary Islands into unknown waters under the command of Christopher Columbus, who was intent on proving that it was possible to reach the Indies by sailing west from Europe.

Land was sighted on October 12, about 33 days after leaving the Canaries, and Columbus claimed the new territory—the Bahamas—for Spain. Thinking he had found the Indies, he named the inhabitants "Indians."

He crossed the Atlantic three more times but it was not until his fourth voyage, in 1502, that he touched on the mainland of America. He finally returned home, rich but disillusioned, in November 1504.

Left A ship of the "Santa Maria" type, used by Columbus on his epic transatlantic voyage in 1492. Only the Santa Maria was fully decked.

Columbus voyage one
August 1492–March 1493

Columbus voyage two
September 1493–June 1496

Columbus voyage three
June–August 1498

Columbus voyage four
May–June 1502

Right Initially relations between the Spanish and the natives of the Caribbean islands were friendly.

Above Columbus claimed the Bahamas for Spain in October 1492. Sailing on, he mistook the island of Cuba for the mainland of China.

EUROPE

SPAIN

PORTUGAL

Palos
Cadiz
Lisbon

AZORES (PORTUGAL)

MADEIRA (PORTUGAL)

CANARY IS. (SPAIN)

AFRICA

Tropic of Cancer

Equator

NORTH ATLANTIC OCEAN

SOUTH ATLANTIC OCEAN

CAPE VERDE ISLANDS

Arctic Circle

CANADA

UNITED STATES OF AMERICA

Boston
New York City
Washington D.C.

New Orleans

Gulf of Mexico

Miami

BERMUDA

THE BAHAMAS

Havana

CUBA

JAMAICA

Santo Domingo

Puerto Rico

DOMINICA

Martinique

Caribbean Sea

Caracas

TRINIDAD

VENEZUELA

COLOMBIA

GUYANA

SURINAM

French Guiana

SOUTH AMERICA

PACIFIC OCEAN

Crossing the new continent

Right *Lewis and Clark's overland route to the Pacific was arduous and dangerous. Harsh winter weather made mountains impassable.*

In the winter of 1803–1804, Captain Meriwether Lewis and his deputy, Lieutenant William Clark, prepared for an epic journey that was to cover 8,000 miles (12,875 km). Their mission was to find an overland route to the Pacific.

The expedition overwintered at the Mandan villages in North Dakota, setting off again on April 7, 1805 with a Shoshoni guide, Sacajawea, carrying her two-month-old baby on her back. They reached the Great Falls of the Missouri in June and hauled their boats and equipment overland.

The group eventually crossed the Rocky Mountains, and accompanied by friendly Nez Percé Indians, they took to the water again, first on the Clearwater River, then on the Snake, and finally on the mighty Columbia. The fast-flowing waters bore them past the site of modern Portland and on to the Pacific coast on November 15, 1805.

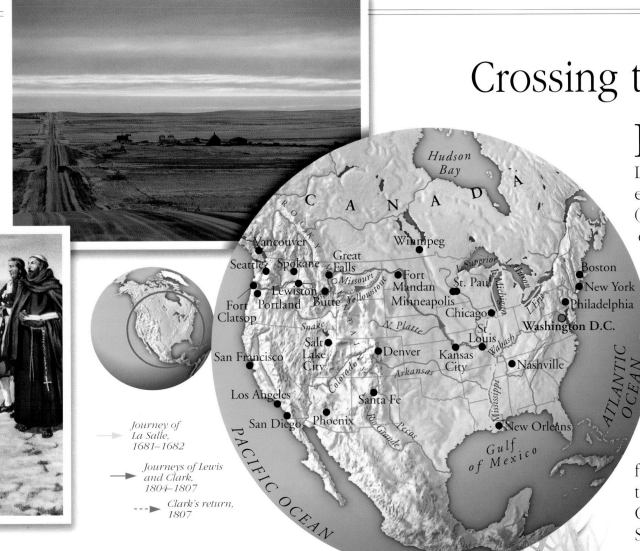

Journey of La Salle, 1681–1682

Journeys of Lewis and Clark, 1804–1807

Clark's return, 1807

Below *La Salle taking possession of "Louisiana."*

FROM THE GREAT LAKES TO THE GULF OF MEXICO

In January 1682, the French explorer Sieur de la Salle traveled from Fort Crevecoeur ("Fort Heartbreak") on the Illinois River to the confluence of the Illinois and the Mississippi. His expedition included 23 fellow Frenchmen, 18 American Indians, and his second-in-command, Henri de Tonti. Their objective was to navigate the entire length of North America's mightiest river. Once the winter ice had broken up in mid-February, the group progressed in canoes meeting friendly Arkansas, Taensa, and Coroa Indians. The successful journey was completed in early April when the travelers reached the Gulf of Mexico and la Salle formally claimed Louisiana (so named in honor of Louis XIV) for France in a ceremony on April 9, 1683.

Right *The West was wilderness, rich in wildlife, some of it very dangerous. On April 7, 1805, Lewis and Clark survived their first encounter with a grizzly bear.*

Right *Meriwether Lewis (1774–1809) and William Clark (1770–1838) whose expedition to the Pacific was sponsored by President Thomas Jefferson.*

11

Northern Territory

Canada is a vast country, and its exploration involved many intrepid travelers and took several centuries. In May 1497, John Cabot was the first documented transatlantic voyager to reach Canada's eastern coast, followed in 1534 by Jacques Cartier who explored the Gulf of St. Lawrence and the St. Lawrence River. In 1535, Cartier reached 1,000 miles (1,600 km) inland, to the site of today's Montreal. In 1608, Samuel de Champlain founded the first permanent French colony in the New World.

In the west, James Cook surveyed the coast in 1778 while searching for the Northwest passage, and in 1792, George Vancouver sailed around the island now called Vancouver. In 1789, Alexander Mackenzie followed the river that now bears his name to the Arctic. In 1793, he was the first European to cross North America by land.

Left *The distinctive totem poles of the Kwakiutl.*

→ Jacques Cartier, 1534

⇢ Jacques Cartier, 1535–1536

→ John Cabot, 1497

→ Samuel Champlain, 1604–1607

→ Alexander Mackenzie, 1789

⇢ Alexander Mackenzie, 1793

→ James Cook, 1778

→ George Vancouver, 1793–1794

Left *In 1793, Scotsman Alexander Mackenzie was the first explorer to prove that the Rockies could be crossed.*

Above *Vikings were notorious warriors who regularly descended on the coasts of Britain, Ireland, and France to raid and trade.*

"VINLAND"

Leif Eriksson was the son of the Viking, Erik the Red, who had established a settlement at Brattahild in southern Greenland. Around AD 1000, Leif Eriksson sailed with a crew of 35 in search of the mysterious land to the west. After sailing for 200 miles (320 km) he reached a place he called Helluland ("land of stone slabs"), probably the southern part of Baffin Island. Then he traveled south to Markland ("land of woods"), now identified as southern Labrador.

Eriksson reached a bountiful country, with rivers full of salmon. One member of the group became tipsy on wild grapes so Leif Eriksson called the land "Vinland" (land of wine). The party spent the winter in Vinland, and were the first Europeans to set foot in North America.

→ Voyage of Leif Eriksson

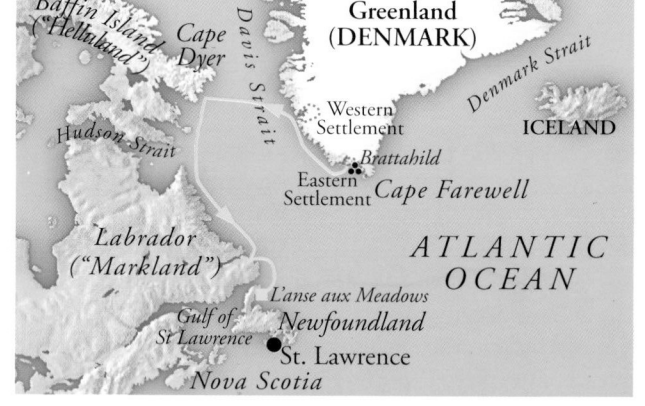

Hernán Cortés, conqueror of Mexico

Invasion route toTenochtitlán, Aug.–Nov. 1519

Conjectural route of forced march to Veracruz, 1520

Cortés's' route to Mexico, 1519–1520

Cortés's' expedition to Honduras, 1524

On February 18, 1519, the Spanish governor of Cuba sent 11 ships commanded by Hernán Cortés to explore the rich mainland empire of the Aztecs ruled over by the mighty Moctezuma II.

The expedition was welcomed by a local Indian chief who complained bitterly about the brutal Aztecs. Cortés marched on the Aztec capital, Tenochtitlán, with thousands of Indian allies. He seized and imprisoned Moctezuma, turning him into a Spanish puppet-ruler. But Cortés was forced to return to Veracruz to confront Spanish troops sent to arrest him and the Aztecs rebelled. On his return Cortés was captured but escaped to Tlaxcala. Cortés laid siege to Tenochtitlán and the starving city finally yielded in 1521. Cortés had conquered the Aztecs.

Above *Although Cortés defeated Moctezuma and won Mexico for Spain, he was never made governor of Mexico.*

Left *The Aztecs sacrificed 50,000 captives a year to the sun and the earth.*

Above *An Aztec mask of turquoise, shell, and wood, representing the much-feared feathered serpent god, Tzalcoatl.*

Right *The Aztecs ruled their empire from the island city of Tenochtitlán on Lake Texcoco.*

Uncharted waters

In 1519, Ferdinand Magellan embarked on a momentous journey to find a western route to Asia.

Magellan's fleet of five ships set off down the coast of South America in October 1520. The fleet soon sighted the straits they had been searching for. For 38 days they headed into strong winds and on November 28, 1520, they entered the unknown waters of the Pacific Ocean.

At least 19 men died during the crossing. Magellan himself was killed in a battle on the island of Mactan. His surviving ships limped on and one eventually reached Spain in September 1522.

Left The Spaniards must have been fascinated by the Patagonian penguins. Unique to the southern hemisphere, they were first seen when Magellan's fleet rounded Cape Horn on the southern tip of South America in November 1520.

Below Magellan's men marveled at Brazil's multicolored parrots.

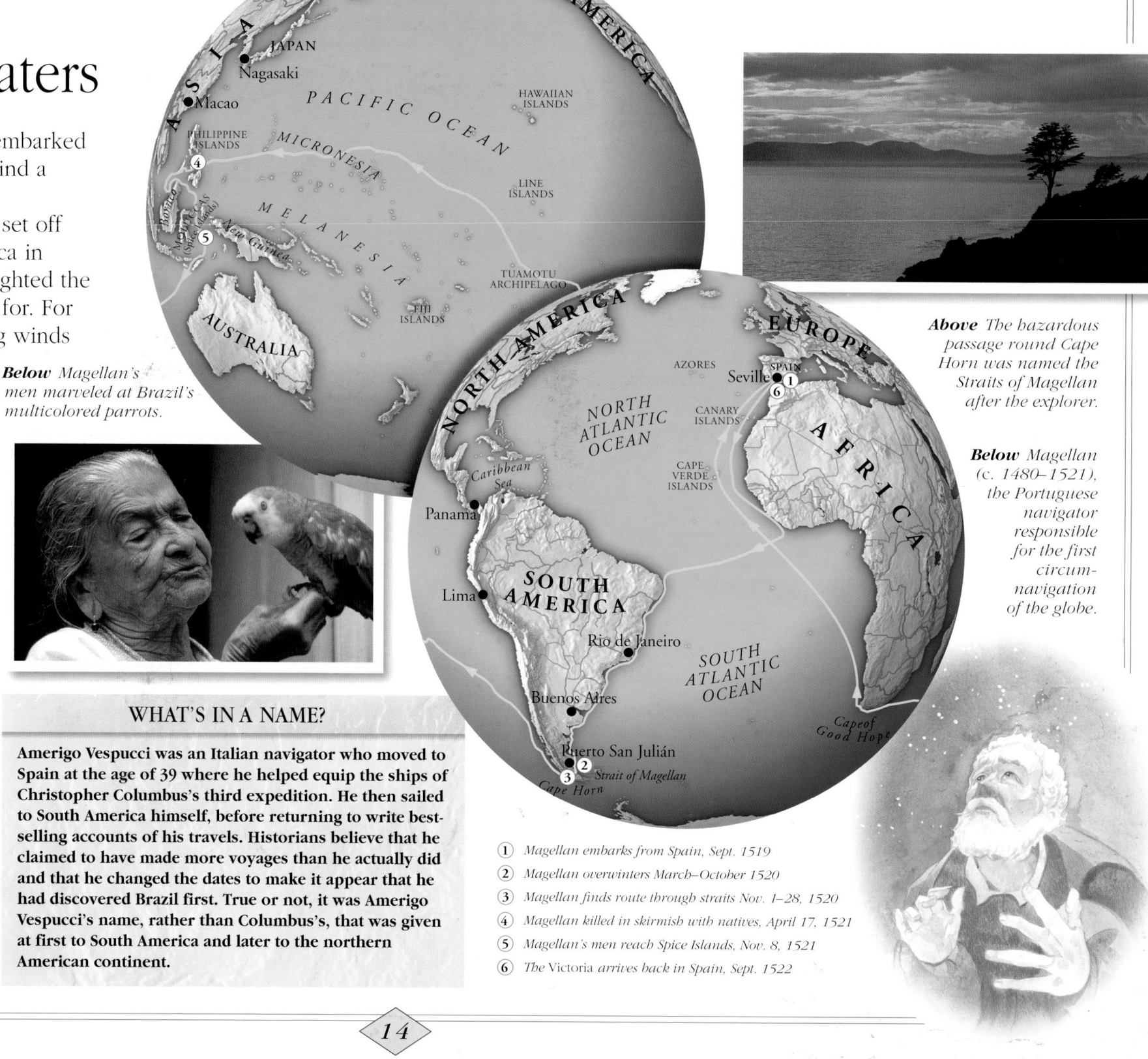

Above The hazardous passage round Cape Horn was named the Straits of Magellan after the explorer.

Below Magellan (c. 1480–1521), the Portuguese navigator responsible for the first circum-navigation of the globe.

WHAT'S IN A NAME?

Amerigo Vespucci was an Italian navigator who moved to Spain at the age of 39 where he helped equip the ships of Christopher Columbus's third expedition. He then sailed to South America himself, before returning to write best-selling accounts of his travels. Historians believe that he claimed to have made more voyages than he actually did and that he changed the dates to make it appear that he had discovered Brazil first. True or not, it was Amerigo Vespucci's name, rather than Columbus's, that was given at first to South America and later to the northern American continent.

① Magellan embarks from Spain, Sept. 1519

② Magellan overwinters March–October 1520

③ Magellan finds route through straits Nov. 1–28, 1520

④ Magellan killed in skirmish with natives, April 17, 1521

⑤ Magellan's men reach Spice Islands, Nov. 8, 1521

⑥ The Victoria arrives back in Spain, Sept. 1522

Conqueror of the Incas

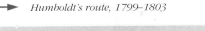
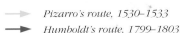

→ Pizarro's route, 1530–1533
→ Humboldt's route, 1799–1803

Above Francisco Pizarro (c. 1475–1541), who defeated the Inca empire with only 185 men.

Below Von Humboldt climbed Chimborazo in Ecuador (19,000 feet/5,790 m), a record at that time.

L ured by stories of Inca gold, Spanish conquistador Francisco Pizarro and a small force of soldiers of fortune arrived at Tumbes in northern Peru in 1532.

Pizarro set off to meet the Inca ruler, Atahuallpa. On November 16, they reached Cajamarca where Atahuallpa and his army of 30,000 awaited them. Pizarro trapped Atahuallpa in the main square and surrounded it with hidden cavalry. The Spaniards attacked with muskets and cannon massacring at least 2,000 Incas. Atahuallpa was captured and produced a massive ransom. When he had served his purpose, however, he was garrotted.

The conquistadors finally took the Inca capital, Cuzco, in November 1533. A tiny but ruthless force had conquered the mightiest empire in South America.

Above The Inca ruler Atahuallpa was brutally murdered by the Spanish.

PASSION FOR ADVENTURE

From 1799 to 1803 Baron Alexander von Humboldt explored Cuba, Colombia, Ecuador, and Peru. He navigated the Orinoco and the Amazon rivers in canoes that often overturned in turbulent or alligator-infested waters. Later, his pet dog, a mastiff, was eaten by a jaguar in the jungle.

Throughout his travels he never shrank from danger even drinking Indian arrow-poison to show it was only lethal when injected in the bloodstream. He also measured earthquakes, climbed volcanoes, and braved altitude sickness and storms to climb Mount Chimborazo in Ecuador, reaching a record-breaking height of 19,000 feet (5,790 m).

Left Alexander von Humboldt (1769–1859), the Prussian natural scientist who traveled to South America.

Descending the Amazon

In 1540, Gonzalo Pizarro (brother of Francisco) set off to survey the densely forested area to the east of Quito. When supplies became short a small party of 60 men, led by Francisco de Orellana, was sent down the Napo River in a two-masted sailing ship in search of food.

They soon reached the Amazon. Orellana decided to drift with the river, hoping to reach the Atlantic Ocean. Over the next nine months, the group fought off countless Indian war parties in canoes. Despite these dangers, after a journey of 3,000 miles (4,825 km), the ship eventually reached the ocean.

Above *On his journey down the mighty Amazon, de Orellana was attacked by fierce female warriors and so he named the river "Amazon" after the mythical women warriors of Ancient Greece.*

...... ▶ *Route of Francisco de Orellana*

① *Orellana sails into the Amazon, February 12, 1542*

② *Orellana encounters warlike Indians, May 12, 1542*

③ *Orellana claims to have fought women warriors, or Amazons, June 24, 1542*

——▶ *1595 Route of Sir Walter Raleigh*

......▶ *1617 Route of Sir Walter Raleigh*

Right *South American gold lured European explorers.*

Right *Sir Walter Raleigh (c. 1554–1618). English adventurer, who founded a colony in Virginia, and explored the Orinoco river in search of El Dorado ("the gilded man"). His search ended in tragedy and the mythical city was never found.*

Right *Amazonian piranhas can strip a man to his bones in minutes.*

EL DORADO

Some explorers are driven by the lure of fabulous riches. Sir Walter Raleigh was such a man. Motivated by the myth of El Dorado ("the gilded man"), Raleigh sailed from England to South America in 1595 to find the fabled inland city of the same name. After losing two of his expedition's ships in Atlantic storms, he and his remaining crew landed in Trinidad before canoeing more than 500 miles (800 km) up the Orinoco. During their arduous journey they were often lost in a maze of streams and tributaries and were finally forced back by the seasonal rains, which turned the river into a raging torrent. In 1617, Raleigh returned to search for El Dorado but was ambushed by the Spanish. His son Wat was killed and Raleigh returned home in disgrace. He never found the mythical golden city.

Above *A 19th-century engraving, based on Whymper's popular account of his Ecuadorean adventures, showing an attempt to pitch camp against driving snow.*

High peaks of the Andes

Route taken by Whymper

△ Peak climbed by Whymper

PACIFIC OCEAN

Cotocachi △ Ibarra
Otavalo ●   ●Cayambe
            △ *Cayambe*
Quito ○   △ *Sara-Urcu*
Corazon △ △ *Antisana*
Illiniza △ △ *Sincholagua*
            Cotopaxi
ECUADOR ● Latacunga
Carihuairazo △ ●Ambata *Napo*
Chimborazo △
Guaranda ●   ●Riobamba
    ● Babahoyo
Guayaquil ●

Gulf of Guayaquil   Cuenca ●

Daule *Vinces*

In 1879, the European mountaineer, Edward Whymper, arrived in Ecuador to pioneer exploration of the Andes.

Whymper headed straight for the mountain of Chimborazo, northeast of Guayaquil. Despite a desperate struggle against altitude sickness he scaled both Chimborazo's western and eastern peaks.

Whymper's party began the ascent of Cotopaxi, the active volcano to the north. The closer they got to the crater's rim, the more the volcanic ash penetrated their ears, eyes, and nostrils. Whymper crawled over to peer down into the volcano at the red, molten lava below.

Whymper conquered many other high peaks, surveying the land and collecting samples of local plants and insects. He also established that altitude sickness is directly related to atmospheric pressure.

Left *The spectacular Inca town of Machu Picchu perches on top of a rugged mountain. Workers smoothed the rock to form flat surfaces on which to build major temples. The steep flanking slopes were terraced to support small thatched houses, as well as for cultivation. Machu Picchu has become one of Peru's main tourist attractions.*

THE INCAS' HIDDEN CITY

When Hiram Bingham, a lecturer in Latin American history at Yale University, set off in 1911 in search of the lost Inca cities of Vilcabamba and Vitcos, little did he know what he would soon discover. Local guides led him to a site high above the Urubamba Valley where he saw "a great flight of beautifully constructed stone-faced terraces, perhaps a hundred of them, each hundreds of feet long and ten feet high." Bingham had found Machu Picchu. Although it has since been shown not to be Vilcabamba or Vitcos, as Bingham believed, Machu Picchu is a breathtaking place that is recognized as one of the architectural wonders of the world.

Left *Hiram Bingham (1875–1956), U.S. archaeologist and explorer of Inca Peru.*

Right *English writer and mountaineer Edward Whymper, (1840–1911).*

Ibn Battuta

In 1325, Ibn Battuta, an Arab from Tangier, in present-day Morocco, decided to embark on a journey to all the holy places of the Muslim world. His travels were to take 30 years.

First, Ibn Battuta explored the ancient cities of the Nile valley. He made the Muslim holy city of Mecca into his second home, using it as a base from which to explore much of the Middle East, Central Asia, and the Muslim states of East Africa.

In 1351, he journeyed south through the Sahara to Mali. Battuta explored the River Niger by canoe and visited the fabled desert city of Timbuktu.

In 1354, he returned home to write *Rihla*, an account of his travels, a fascinating insight into one of the medieval world's greatest explorers.

Above Zheng Ho returned from his African voyage with a giraffe—an object of great curiosity in China.

Right The construction of larger ocean-going vessels was banned after Zheng Ho's voyages to east Africa, when Ming China became isolationist and inward-looking.

→ Journeys of Ibn Battuta 1325–1354

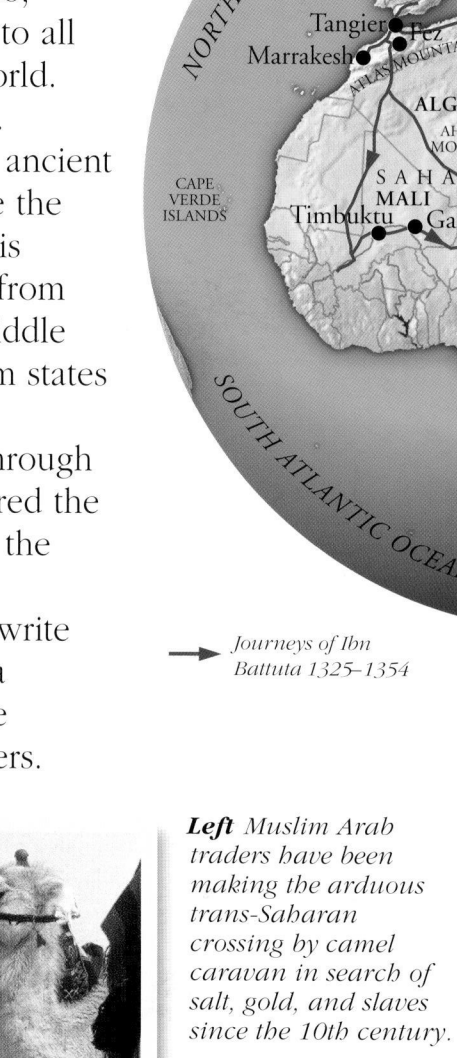

Left Muslim Arab traders have been making the arduous trans-Saharan crossing by camel caravan in search of salt, gold, and slaves since the 10th century.

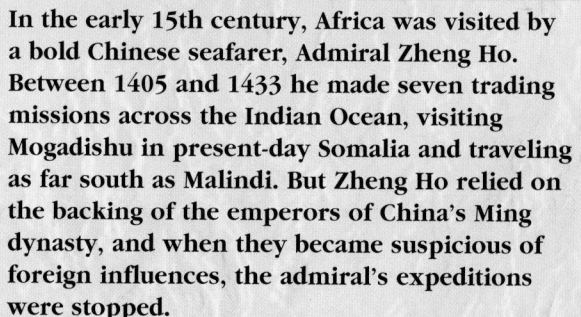
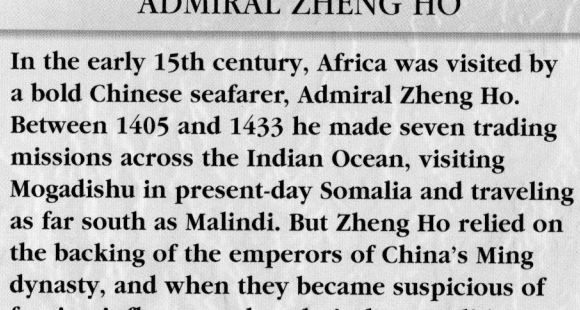

Right There was a flourishing trade in Chinese porcelain in the 15th century.

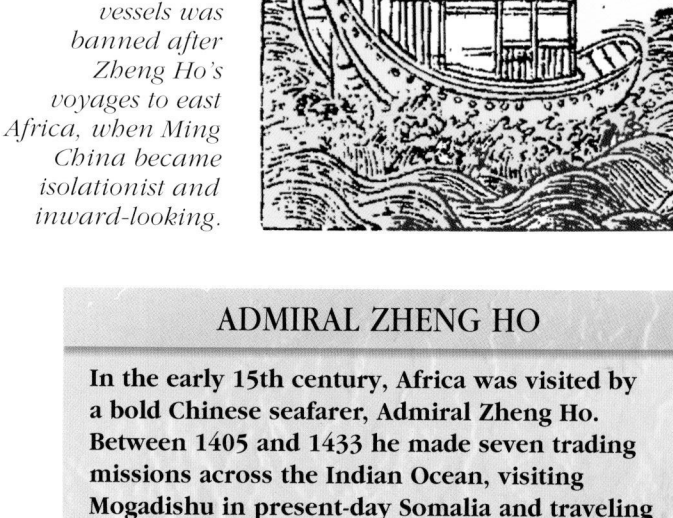

ADMIRAL ZHENG HO

In the early 15th century, Africa was visited by a bold Chinese seafarer, Admiral Zheng Ho. Between 1405 and 1433 he made seven trading missions across the Indian Ocean, visiting Mogadishu in present-day Somalia and traveling as far south as Malindi. But Zheng Ho relied on the backing of the emperors of China's Ming dynasty, and when they became suspicious of foreign influences, the admiral's expeditions were stopped.

The source of the Nile

The Nile, the world's longest river, flows for 3,500 miles (5,630 km) through Sudan and Egypt. But in the mid-19th century its origin was a mystery. In 1856, celebrated explorer Richard Burton accompanied by John Hanning Speke, an ex-soldier and big game hunter, set off from Zanzibar to find the source of the Nile. Having overcome desperate fevers and rebellious porters they discovered Lake Tanganyika, but realized it could not be the source of the Nile.

Speke headed on alone in search of a lake known by locals as Lake Ukerewe. After 25 days of hard trekking, he reached it and named it Lake Victoria. This, he believed, was the source of the Nile. Burton was skeptical, but Speke returned to England a hero. Two years later, he reached Lake Victoria again. He traced the Nile to the lake's northern end, and sent a triumphant telegram: "The Nile is settled."

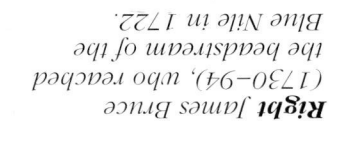

Right James Bruce (1730-94), who reached the headstream of the Blue Nile in 1722.

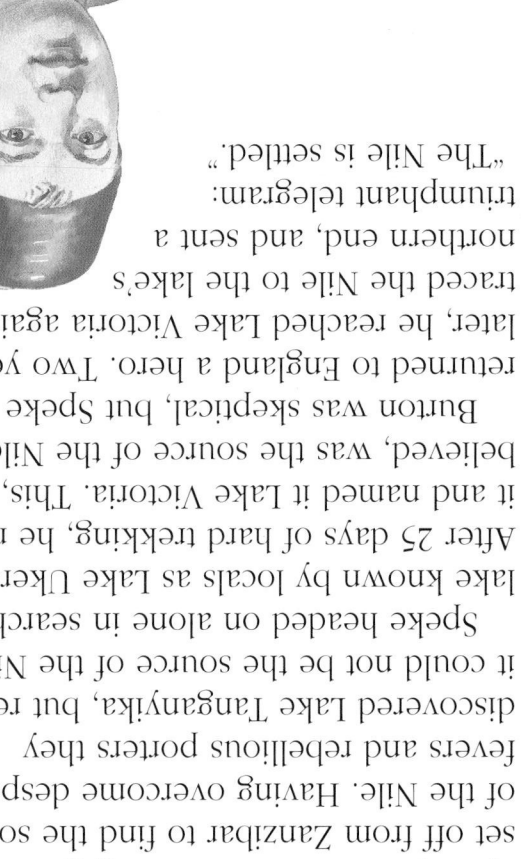

Left John Hanning Speke (1827-94), English soldier and explorer who discovered the headwaters of the River Nile

Right Sir Richard Francis Burton (1821-90), British linguist, writer, and explorer of Saudi Arabia and Lake Tanganyika

Above Lake Victoria, source of the River Nile, is the second-largest freshwater body in the world. It is approximately 250 miles (400 km) long. It was explored by J.H. Speke in 1858, and again with J.A. Grant, in 1862.

← Route of Richard Burton and John Speke, 1856-59

← Route of John Speke, 1858

← Route of John Speke and James Grant, 1860-63

Speke and Grant rendezvous with porters and proceed to Khartoum

Right Dinka dancer in southern Sudan playing a horn.

Africa, from coast to coast

S cottish explorer David Livingstone was a medical doctor and missionary who arrived in Karuma (Botswana) in 1841. Frustrated by his missionary activities, he turned to exploration.

Crossing the Kalahari Desert in 1849, he visited Lake Ngami. Eventually he came to the Zambezi River in 1851, and in 1856, after an exhausting 21-month journey, he became the first European to cross Africa.

In 1866, he set out to find the sources of the Nile and the Congo. For five years he lost contact with Europeans. When reporter Henry Stanley found him on Lake Tanganyika, he met him with the famous words, "Doctor Livingstone, I presume."

Above *David Livingstone (1813–73), Scottish explorer of Africa.*

Right *David Livingstone was mauled by a lion at Mabotosa in southern Africa, but this did not deter him from his travels.*

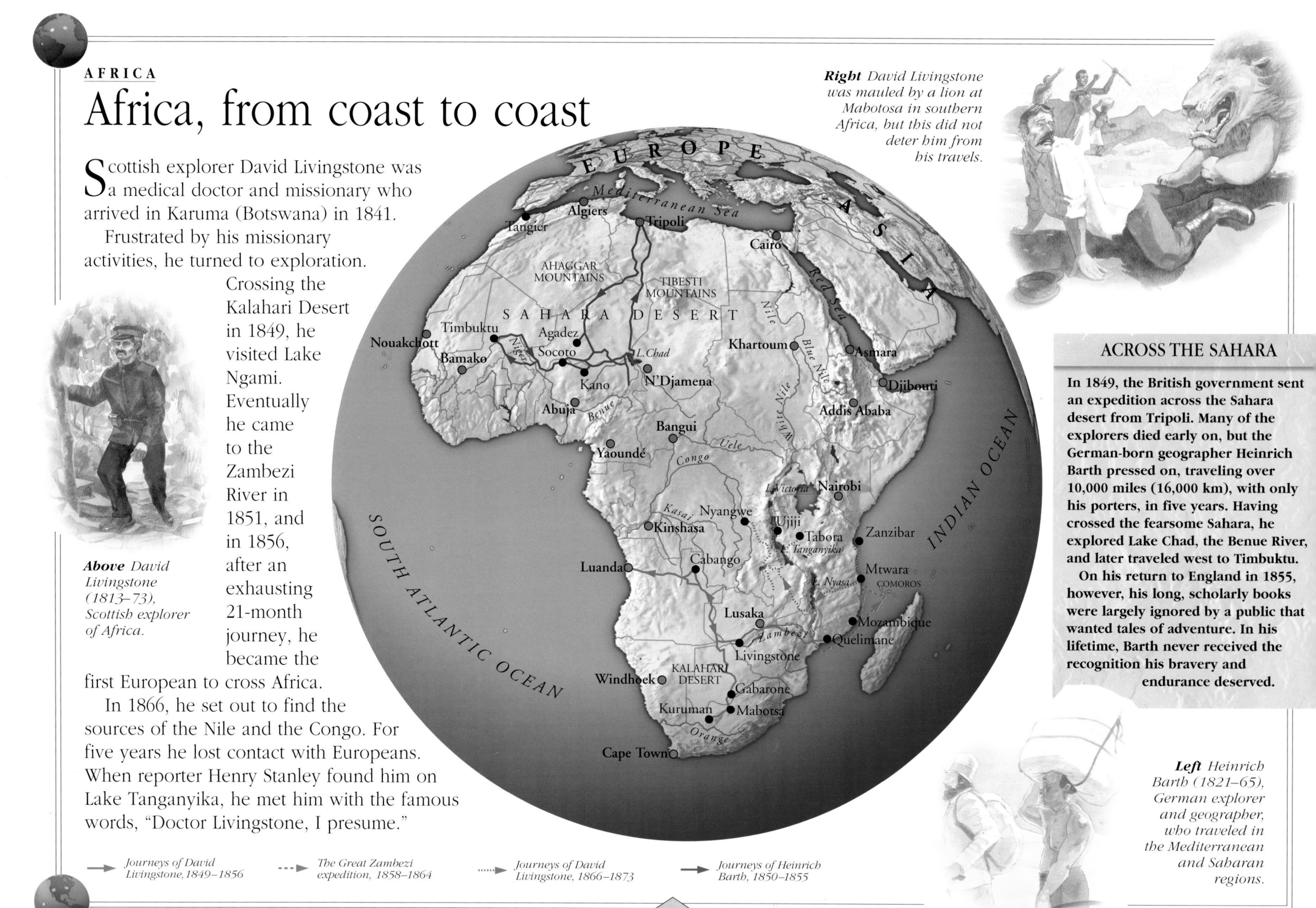

ACROSS THE SAHARA

In 1849, the British government sent an expedition across the Sahara desert from Tripoli. Many of the explorers died early on, but the German-born geographer Heinrich Barth pressed on, traveling over 10,000 miles (16,000 km), with only his porters, in five years. Having crossed the fearsome Sahara, he explored Lake Chad, the Benue River, and later traveled west to Timbuktu.

On his return to England in 1855, however, his long, scholarly books were largely ignored by a public that wanted tales of adventure. In his lifetime, Barth never received the recognition his bravery and endurance deserved.

Left *Heinrich Barth (1821–65), German explorer and geographer, who traveled in the Mediterranean and Saharan regions.*

→ *Journeys of David Livingstone, 1849–1856*

---→ *The Great Zambezi expedition, 1858–1864*

......→ *Journeys of David Livingstone, 1866–1873*

→ *Journeys of Heinrich Barth, 1850–1855*

A Woman in West Africa

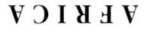

Although the first coastal map of West Africa was made by Diogo Cão in 1482, early explorers made few journeys inland until 1874, when Henry Stanley descended the great Congo River as far as Boma on the Atlantic Ocean. Englishwoman Mary Kingsley left for Africa in 1893 with little more than a bag of books and blankets. She sailed up the Congo River and traveled in the interior, trading tobacco and collecting specimens of insects and fish. In 1894, she made a second journey to Gabon. She canoed up the crocodile-infested Ogooué River and spent a terrifying night with the Fang cannibals. She became the first woman to climb Mount Cameroon.

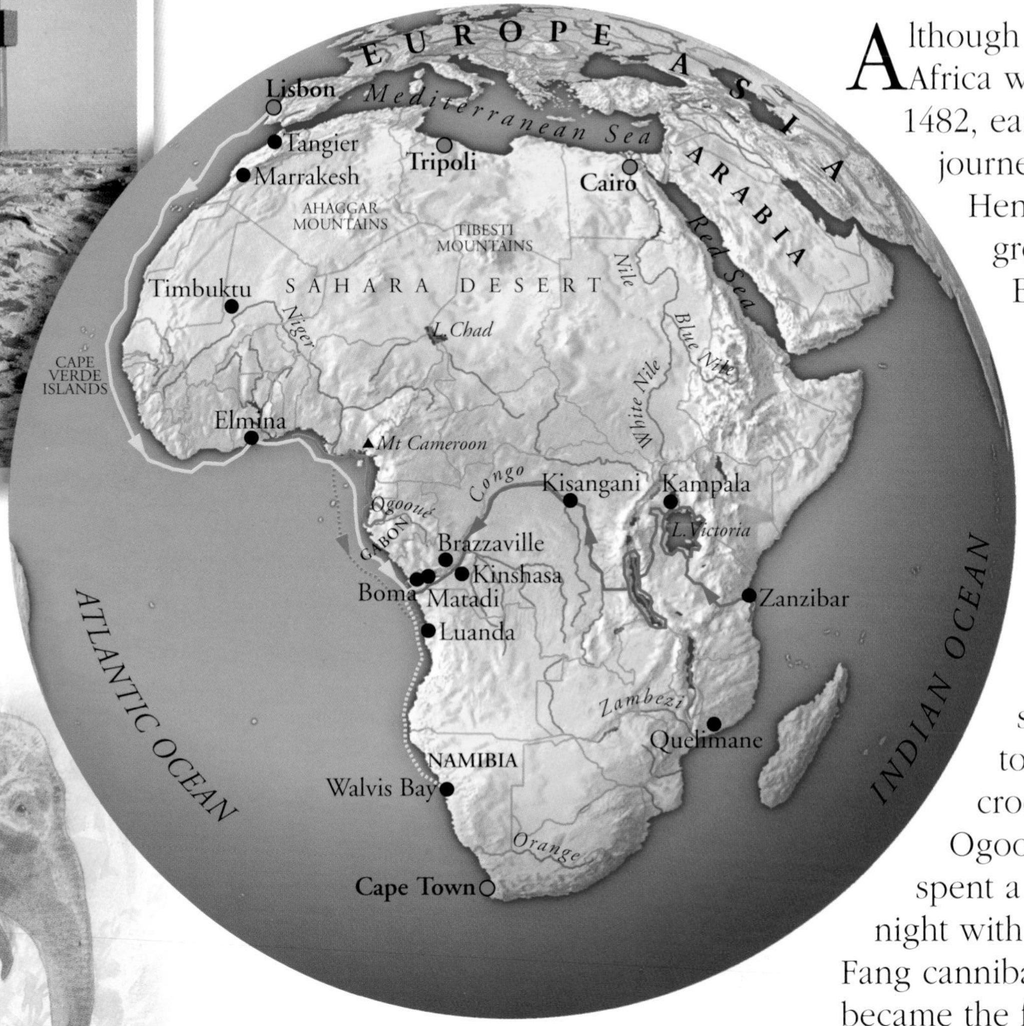

Right Mary Kingsley (1862–1900), the English traveler who journeyed through western Africa and became the first European to visit Gabon.

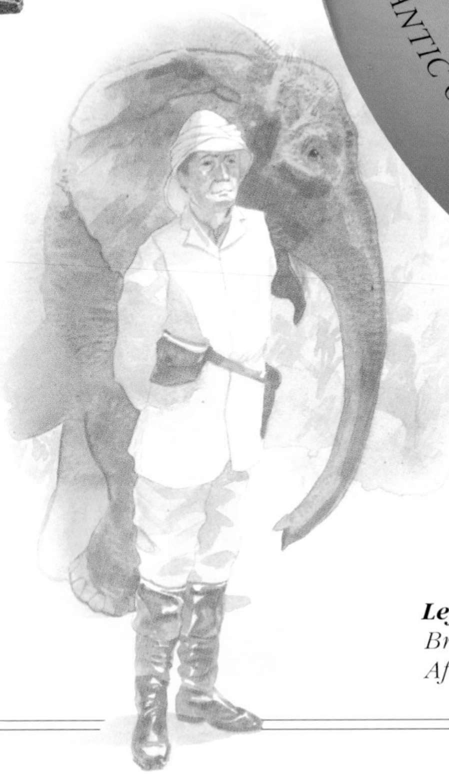

Left Henry Morton Stanley (1841–1904), British-American explorer of central Africa, especially the Congo region.

----- Journey of Mary Kingsley, 1894

⟵ Journey of Mary Kingsley, 1893

⟵ Journey of Henry Stanley, 1874–1879

◁ ◁ Explorations of Diogo Cão, 1485

◁ ◁ Explorations of Diogo Cão, 1482

Left The stone tablet and cross in honor of Diogo Cão, the first European to arrive in Namibia in 1482.

Left The brass sculptures of the West African civilization of Benin are famous. This armed Portuguese soldier dates from the 17th century.

Map labels: EUROPE, ASIA, ARABIA, ATLANTIC OCEAN, INDIAN OCEAN, CAPE VERDE ISLANDS, Lisbon, Tangier, Marrakesh, Tripoli, Cairo, Mediterranean Sea, Red Sea, SAHARA DESERT, TIBESTI MOUNTAINS, AHAGGAR MOUNTAINS, Timbuktu, L. Chad, Niger, Nile, Blue Nile, White Nile, Mt Cameroon, Elmina, Ogooué, Congo, Kisangani, Kampala, L. Victoria, Brazzaville, Kinshasa, Boma, Matadi, Luanda, Zanzibar, Quelimane, Zambezi, NAMIBIA, Walvis Bay, Orange, Cape Town

Continent in the south

In 1769, Captain James Cook embarked on his first voyage to the South Seas when he sailed to Tahiti. He then turned south and sighted New Zealand. At a place he named Poverty Bay he was attacked by Maoris. In April 1770, he became the first European to see the eastern coast of Australia and, on August 21, 1770, he took possession of the eastern half for the British Crown.

On his later voyages, Cook journeyed from the Gulf of Alaska to Antarctica gathering detailed information on natural history, cartography, and meteorology.

On St. Valentine's Day 1779, Cook and his crew fell into an argument with some native people in Hawaii. Cook was surprised and stabbed to death by a local chieftain.

THE REAL ROBINSON CRUSOE

William Dampier was a British navigator and buccaneer who specialized in looting Spanish galleons, and mapped Australia and New Guinea in three voyages between 1679 and 1711. The real-life story of one of his crew members, Alexander Selkirk, was the inspiration for Daniel Defoe's *Robinson Crusoe*. Selkirk apparently disliked Dampier so much that he insisted on being put ashore on the uninhabited island of Juan Fernandez, about 400 miles (643 km) west of Chile, during Dampier's fourth voyage. He then began to scrape an existence on the barren island. But when rescued four years and four months later by Dampier's ship, Selkirk is said to have been difficult to persuade aboard, such were his continued feelings of resentment!

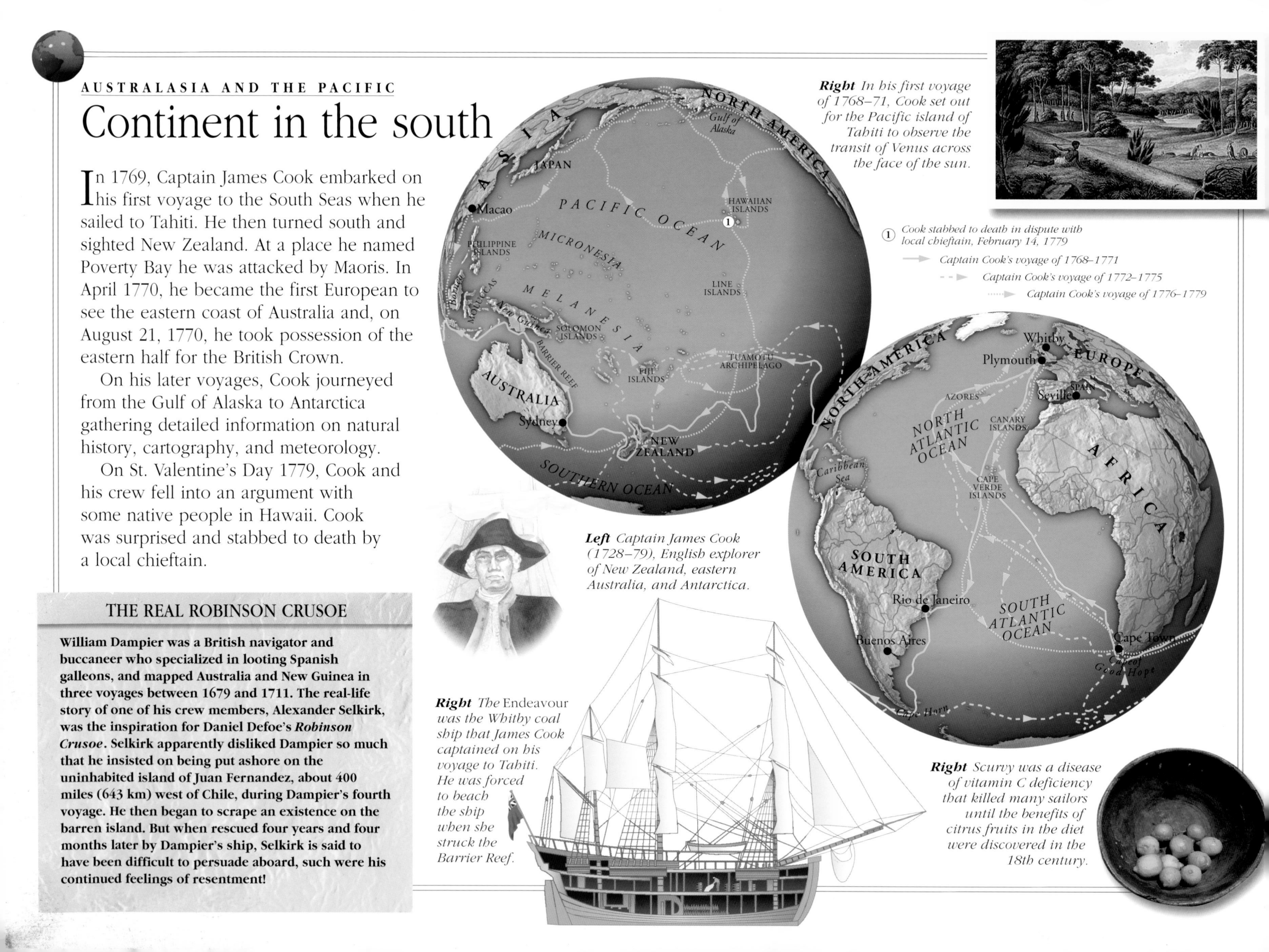

Right In his first voyage of 1768–71, Cook set out for the Pacific island of Tahiti to observe the transit of Venus across the face of the sun.

① Cook stabbed to death in dispute with local chieftain, February 14, 1779

→ Captain Cook's voyage of 1768–1771

--→ Captain Cook's voyage of 1772–1775

·····→ Captain Cook's voyage of 1776–1779

Left Captain James Cook (1728–79), English explorer of New Zealand, eastern Australia, and Antarctica.

Right The Endeavour was the Whitby coal ship that James Cook captained on his voyage to Tahiti. He was forced to beach the ship when she struck the Barrier Reef.

Right Scurvy was a disease of vitamin C deficiency that killed many sailors until the benefits of citrus fruits in the diet were discovered in the 18th century.

The red country

In 1860, after several failed attempts, the citizens of Melbourne sponsored an expedition to traverse the country led by Robert O'Hara Burke and William John Wills. The party of 17 men started out in a blaze of publicity and expectation. Soon things began to go wrong. Carts ground to a halt in mud. Rats devoured the provisions. Burke decided to form a party of four to press on to the north coast, arranging to meet the main expedition at Cooper's Creek, 400 miles (643 km) into the interior.

Struggling through heat, flies, and sandstorms, and surviving on dried horse and camel meat, the party made it to the mangrove swamps near the northern coast in February 1861. They could not penetrate the swamps and turned back, emaciated and in rags, to Cooper's Creek. No one was there to meet them and Burke and Wills died in June 1861 at Cooper's Creek.

Below William Wills (1834–61), English explorer who accompanied Burke on his Australian expedition.

Above Robert Burke (1821–61), Irish explorer who led the trans-Australian expedition.

Right Camels were shipped from India for the desert journey, but they fought with each other and with the horses.

Left European explorers found the Outback harsh and unyielding.

Right Many European expeditions to Australia relied on the bushcraft and hardiness of the Aborigines. They acted as guides, pointing out water sources, and hunting for food.

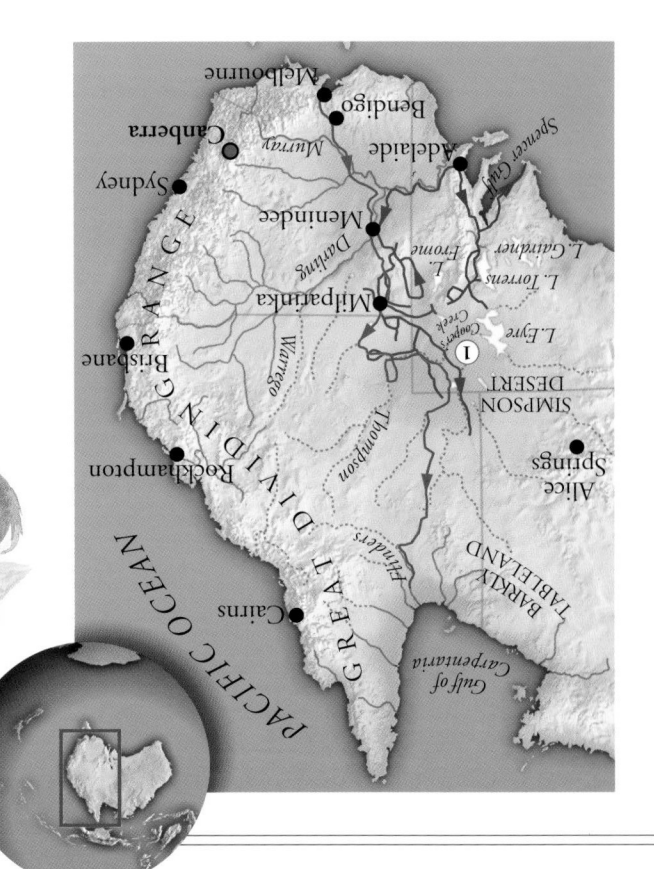

① Burke and Wills die here on their return journey, 1861

← Journeys of Robert Burke and William Wills, 1860–1861

← Journeys of Charles Sturt, 1844–1845

← Journeys of Edward Eyre, 1840

The pioneering Dutch

→ *Abel Tasman's Pacific voyage, 1642*

By the early 17th century, the Dutch were dominating the spice trade in the East Indies establishing a commercial empire based in Batavia (Jakarta). The more southerly regions, including the west coast of Australia, had been encountered mainly by accident, when ships were blown off course.

In 1642, a sea captain named Abel Tasman was hired by the governor of Batavia to explore the commercial opportunities of the "Southland." Tasman sailed from Mauritius to the island he called Van Diemen's Land (now Tasmania) at the southern tip of Australia.

Turning east, Tasman was the first European to sight New Zealand. After a violent clash with the Maoris, he sailed northward becoming the first to visit the Pacific islands of Tonga and Fiji.

Right These giant statues of human heads on Easter Island, are four to five times the height of a child.

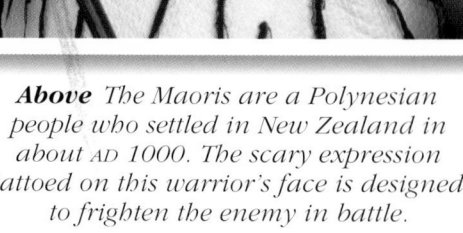

Above Tasman's sketches of Maori war canoes record his violent first encounter with Maoris at the place he named "Murderers' Bay," where four of his crew were killed.

LANDFALL AT EASTER ISLAND

In 1722, Jacob Roggeveen, still looking for the great "Southland," sailed into the Pacific from the coast of Chile. On Easter Day he struck land, naming it Easter Island, and was amazed by the giant monolithic statues of human heads (*moai*) he found there, some up to 32 feet (9.75 m) high. Even today, scientists are unsure about the meaning or purpose of the statues and are only able to tell us that they are the work of a neolithic culture that has since disappeared. One theory goes that the culture vanished following an ecological catastrophe on the island.

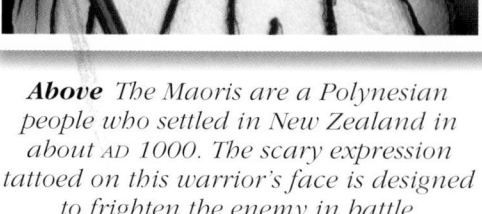

Above The Maoris are a Polynesian people who settled in New Zealand in about AD 1000. The scary expression tattooed on this warrior's face is designed to frighten the enemy in battle.

24

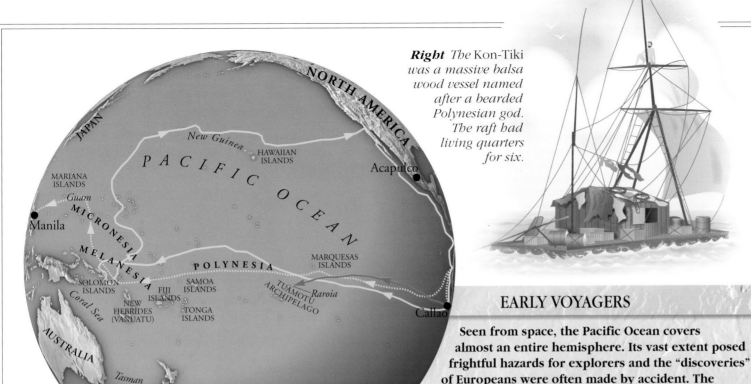

Right *The Kon-Tiki was a massive balsa wood vessel named after a bearded Polynesian god. The raft had living quarters for six.*

Going west

I n the late 1930s, Thor Heyerdahl, a Norwegian living in the Marquesas Islands, developed the theory that the islands of the Pacific had originally been populated not from Asia, but from South America. He decided to try and sail from Peru to the Marquesas using only the materials that would have been available to ancient South American peoples.

In Callao Harbor, Peru, he constructed a massive balsa wood vessel, the *Kon-Tiki*, with living quarters for six men to make the 4,000-mile (6,435-km) journey. They took books, provisions, cinema film, scientific instruments, and a parrot.

Within 97 days, they reached an uninhabited island near Raroia in the Tuamotu group. After several weeks they were taken aboard a French schooner and back to a world eager for news. Heyerdahl's book became a bestseller.

Above *Thor Heyerdahl (born 1914), ethnologist and adventurer, who has reconstructed a number of historical voyages.*

EARLY VOYAGERS

Seen from space, the Pacific Ocean covers almost an entire hemisphere. Its vast extent posed frightful hazards for explorers and the "discoveries" of Europeans were often made by accident. The Marquesas Islands, for example, were first visited in 1595 by the Spanish adventurer Alvaro de Mendaña, but were not found again for almost 200 years. Difficulties with calculating longitude meant that reliable maps were near-impossible and islands were discovered and named more than once by a variety of European powers. Of course, the work had already been done centuries before by the Polynesians, the native peoples of the Pacific, who were highly skilled navigators. Sailing by the stars, voyaging in double-hulled canoes and other smaller craft, they settled the entire hemisphere.

→ *Voyages of Alvaro de Meṅdana, 1567–1569*
⋯ *Voyages of Alvaro de Meṅdana, 1595–1596*
➜ *Kon-Tiki expedition of Thor Heyerdahl*

Below *Thor Heyerdahl constructed the Ra, using only those materials that would have been available to the ancient South American peoples.*

Left *Alvaro de Mendaña was the first European to discover the remote Marquesas Islands in 1595, some centuries after the Polynesians.*

Arctic waters

As trade between Europe and the East Indies increased in the 16th and 17th centuries, the search for a Northwest passage between the Atlantic and Pacific began. A succession of explorers attempted to find a route through the Arctic waters.

In 1903, the Norwegian explorer, Roald Amundsen, set out in his ship *Gjöa* to navigate a way through the islands north of Canada. It took him two and a half years to negotiate the route to the Pacific, proving that it was not a practical seaway.

Below In 1871, 275 years after his Arctic journey, the winter camp of William Barents was found preserved in the snow, exactly as it had been left.

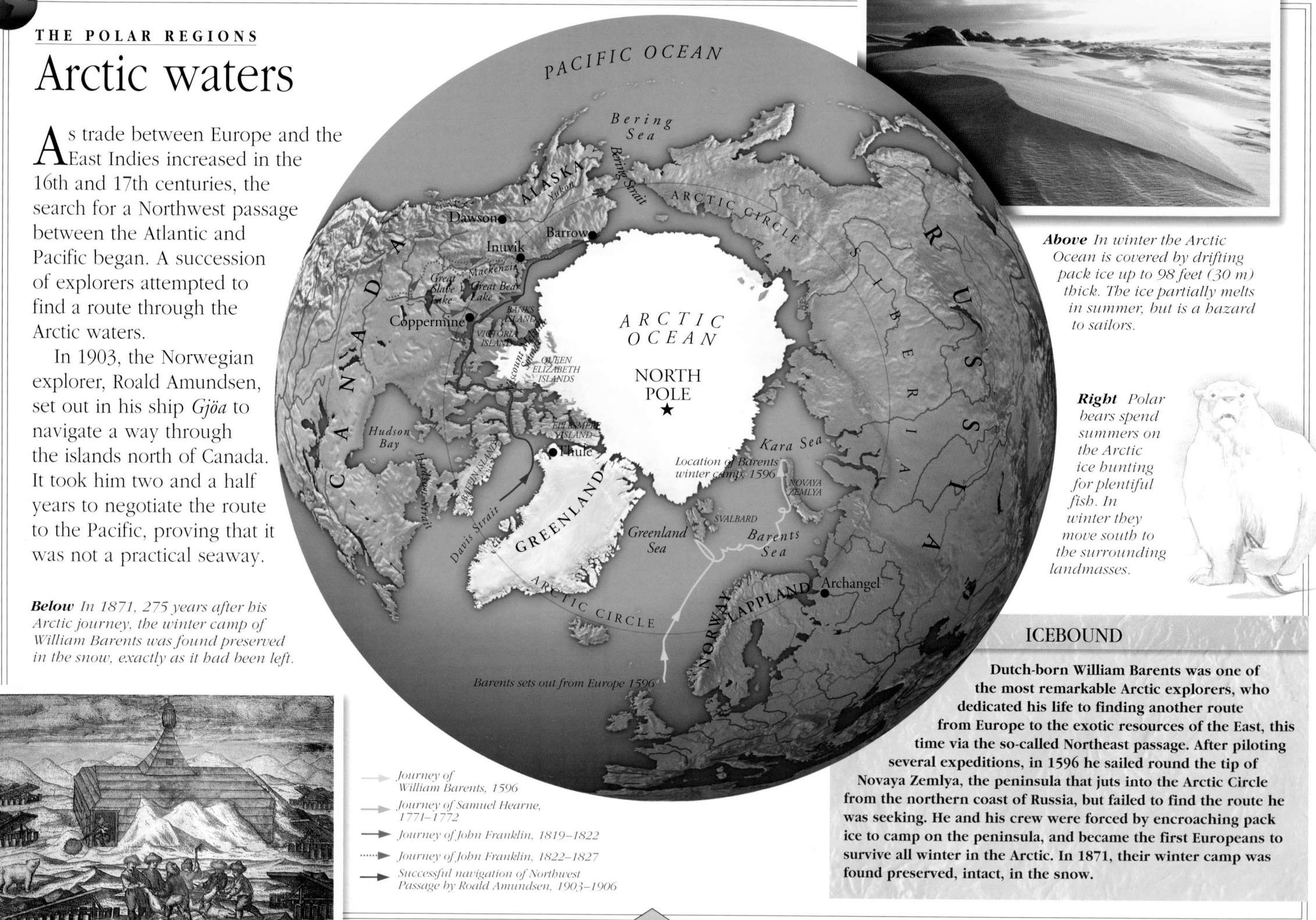

Above In winter the Arctic Ocean is covered by drifting pack ice up to 98 feet (30 m) thick. The ice partially melts in summer, but is a hazard to sailors.

Right Polar bears spend summers on the Arctic ice hunting for plentiful fish. In winter they move south to the surrounding landmasses.

→ Journey of William Barents, 1596
→ Journey of Samuel Hearne, 1771–1772
→ Journey of John Franklin, 1819–1822
····▶ Journey of John Franklin, 1822–1827
→ Successful navigation of Northwest Passage by Roald Amundsen, 1903–1906

ICEBOUND

Dutch-born William Barents was one of the most remarkable Arctic explorers, who dedicated his life to finding another route from Europe to the exotic resources of the East, this time via the so-called Northeast passage. After piloting several expeditions, in 1596 he sailed round the tip of Novaya Zemlya, the peninsula that juts into the Arctic Circle from the northern coast of Russia, but failed to find the route he was seeking. He and his crew were forced by encroaching pack ice to camp on the peninsula, and became the first Europeans to survive all winter in the Arctic. In 1871, their winter camp was found preserved, intact, in the snow.

ARCTIC OCEAN

NORTH POLE

Fort Conger

Cape Columbia

PEARY LAND

GREENLAND

Eureka

AXEL HEIBERG ISLAND

ELLESMERE ISLAND

Kane Basin

Independence Fjord

Bowdoin Bay

Red Cliff House

Dundas

Baffin Bay

→ Peary's expedition to the North Pole, 1892

→ Peary's expedition to the North Pole, 1895

→ Peary's expedition to the North Pole, 1898–1902

→ Successful route to the Pole, 1909

The race to the North Pole

Above *After several unsuccessful Arctic expeditions, Robert Peary reached the North Pole on April 6, 1909.*

Below *The Inuit have survived the harsh terrain and year-round sub-zero temperatures of the Arctic for thousands of years.*

Left *The race between Peary and Cook to become the first man to reach the Pole was the subject of many popular cartoons.*

Above *Frederick Cook, Peary's former assistant, later claimed he had reached the Pole a year earlier.*

A t the end of the 19th century, the North Pole was among the few unexplored places on the globe.

A U.S. naval officer called Robert Peary made it his life's goal to be the first man to reach the Pole. He spent decades training and preparing for his goal.

Successive expeditions were dogged by disaster— hurricanes, a tidal wave, and endless disagreements. On the third attempt, a dash for the Pole resulted in frostbite, and Peary recounted the terrible experience of taking off his boots and leaving parts of his toes behind.

In March 1909 Peary was at last ready to make his final bid for glory, striking out north from Cape Columbia with the loyal support of his Inuit teams. He reached and claimed the North Pole on April 6, 1909.

Right *Robert Peary (1856–1920), the American Arctic explorer, whose obssession with reaching the North Pole was to dominate his life.*

Shackleton and the South Pole

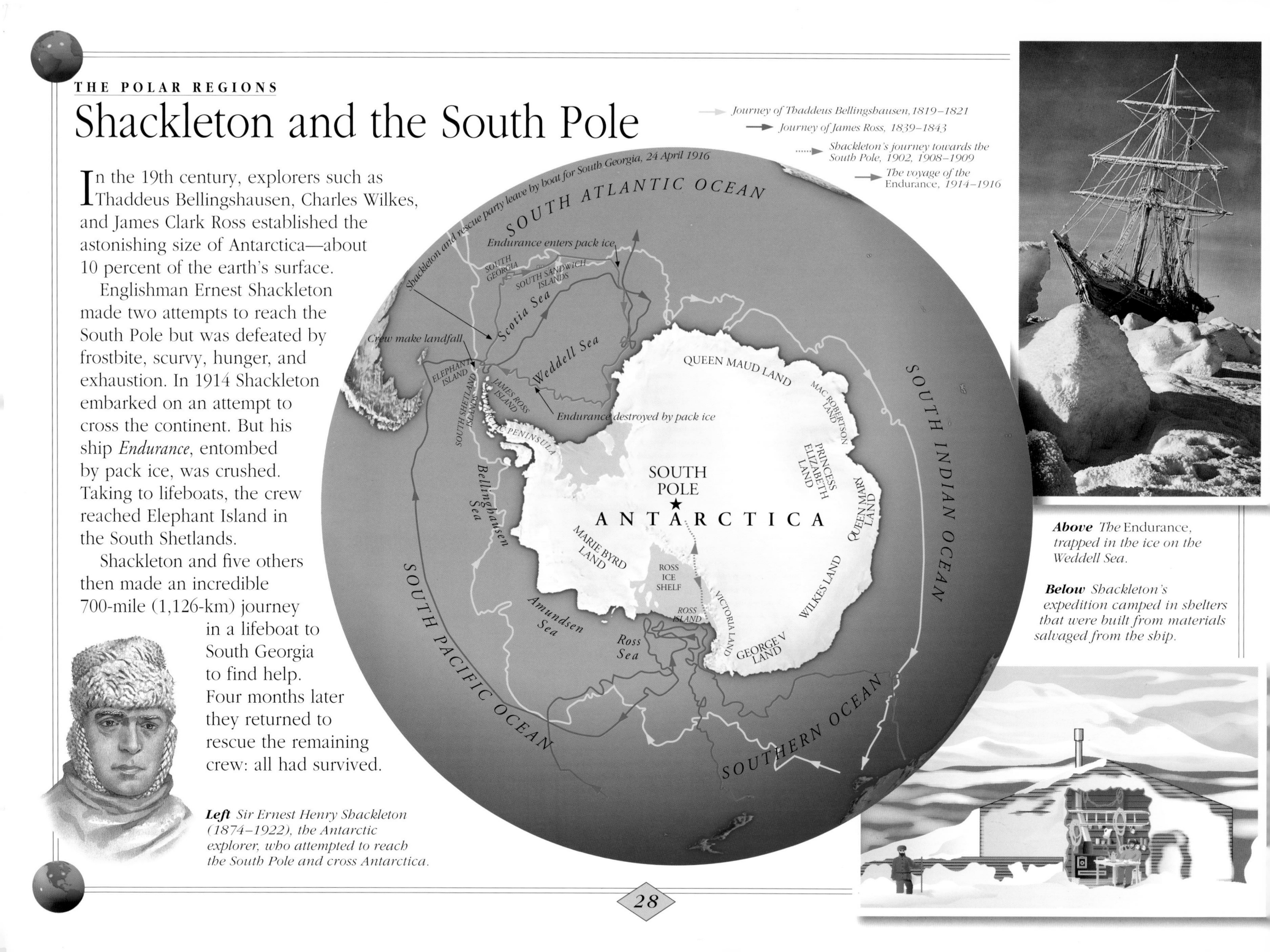

In the 19th century, explorers such as Thaddeus Bellingshausen, Charles Wilkes, and James Clark Ross established the astonishing size of Antarctica—about 10 percent of the earth's surface.

Englishman Ernest Shackleton made two attempts to reach the South Pole but was defeated by frostbite, scurvy, hunger, and exhaustion. In 1914 Shackleton embarked on an attempt to cross the continent. But his ship *Endurance*, entombed by pack ice, was crushed. Taking to lifeboats, the crew reached Elephant Island in the South Shetlands.

Shackleton and five others then made an incredible 700-mile (1,126-km) journey in a lifeboat to South Georgia to find help. Four months later they returned to rescue the remaining crew: all had survived.

Left *Sir Ernest Henry Shackleton (1874–1922), the Antarctic explorer, who attempted to reach the South Pole and cross Antarctica.*

Journey of Thaddeus Bellingshausen, 1819–1821
Journey of James Ross, 1839–1843
Shackleton's journey towards the South Pole, 1902, 1908–1909
The voyage of the Endurance, 1914–1916

Shackleton and rescue party leave by boat for South Georgia, 24 April 1916

SOUTH ATLANTIC OCEAN

Endurance enters pack ice

SOUTH GEORGIA
SOUTH SANDWICH ISLANDS

Scotia Sea

Crew make landfall

Weddell Sea

ELEPHANT ISLAND
SOUTH SHETLAND ISLANDS
JAMES ROSS ISLAND

QUEEN MAUD LAND

Endurance destroyed by pack ice

MAC ROBERTSON LAND

C. PENINSULA

Bellingshausen Sea

SOUTH POLE
★

PRINCESS ELIZABETH LAND

A N T A R C T I C A

SOUTH INDIAN OCEAN

QUEEN MARY LAND

MARIE BYRD LAND

ROSS ICE SHELF

WILKES LAND

SOUTH PACIFIC OCEAN

Amundsen Sea

ROSS ISLAND

VICTORIA LAND

Ross Sea

GEORGE V LAND

SOUTHERN OCEAN

Above *The* Endurance, *trapped in the ice on the Weddell Sea.*

Below *Shackleton's expedition camped in shelters that were built from materials salvaged from the ship.*

Above *The Norwegian explorer Roald Amundsen who reached the South Pole in 1911.*

Above *The British explorer Robert Scott who reached the South Pole in 1912 but died in the attempt.*

Below *The harsh climate of Antarctica makes it uninhabitable. The continent is covered by an ice sheet 1.2 miles (2 km) thick and the surrounding seas are frozen.*

SOUTH POLE

HORLICK MOUNTAINS

TRANSANTARCTIC MOUNTAINS

QUEEN MAUD MOUNTAINS

ANTARCTICA

Scott Glacier
Amundsen Glacier
Axel Heiberg Glacier

Beardmore Glacier

ROSS ICE SHELF

Scott's last camp, located 11 miles (18km) from a food store

Framheim

ROSS ISLAND · Cape Evans

ROOSEVELT ISLAND

McMurdo Sound

Ross Sea

→ Expedition of Roald Amundsen, 1911–1912

→ Expedition of Robert Falcon Scott, 1911–1912

Center of the southern ice

In June 1910, the Norwegian explorer Roald Amundsen set off for Antarctica. His goal was to reach the South Pole. He set up a base (Framheim) on the Ross Ice Shelf and spent the winter laying down supplies. Meanwhile, a rival British expedition, under the command of Robert Falcon Scott, had arrived at the other side of the Ross Ice Shelf at Cape Evans.

In October, Amundsen started off on an unexplored route over difficult country scarred with crevasses. After a 1,400-mile (2,250-km) journey the five-man team reached the Pole on December 14, 1911.

Meanwhile Scott struggled to the pole, reaching it on January 17, 1912. On the return journey the party was delayed by bad weather and the sickness of two of the men, Lawrence Oates and Edgar Evans. Oates sacrificed his life by walking into the blizzard, but in vain. The remaining four died near One·Ton Depot at the end of March.

Above *Amundsen's two-month dash to the Pole, by dog sleds and skis, involved pioneering a route up the Axel Heiberg glacier to the polar plateau.*

SPACE

First man in space

People have long dreamed of voyaging to the stars but it was not until October 4, 1957, when the Soviet Union launched the first satellite, *Sputnik 1*, to orbit the earth that the space age actually began.

Then came the sensational news that Yuri Gagarin, a 27-year-old Soviet cosmonaut, was the first man in space. His flight around the earth, on April 12, 1961, lasted 108 minutes reaching a maximum altitude of 187 miles (300 km). He landed back in the Soviet Union to a hero's welcome.

Above *Yuri Gagarin (1934–68), the Russian cosmonaut and first man in space.*

Below *In April 1961 an R-7 rocket lifted off from the Baikonur Space Center in Kazakhstan and put the spaceship Vostok 1 into orbit. Inside was Gagarin.*

Right *Sputnik 1, launched in October 1957, was a small sphere, weighing only 183 lb (83 kg) and 22 inches (56 cm) in diameter. Sputnik 2 launched a dog, Laika, into orbit but it died after a week.*

Man on the moon

Right *Armstrong and Aldrin spent two hours on the moon's surface, collecting samples of dust and rock, and taking photographs. These samples have been invaluable for scientific research.*

Left *A space shuttle is an aircraft that can make repeated flights in space. The American space shuttle uses huge booster rockets to launch it into orbit.*

President Kennedy committed the United States to putting a man on the moon by the end of the 1960s.

On July 16, 1969, a Saturn rocket took off from Florida at the start of a 240,000-mile (386,000-km) journey. At 120 miles (193 km) above the earth, the command module *Columbia* was thrust out of the earth's gravitational pull and was on course for the moon.

On July 20, Neil Armstrong and Edwin (Buzz) Aldrin entered the lunar module, *Apollo 11*. When the module touched down Armstrong became the first man on the moon, saying "That's one small step for man, one giant leap for mankind."

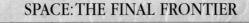

SPACE: THE FINAL FRONTIER

Humans are continually seeking new frontiers, and the exploration of space is no exception. Who knows, science fiction may well become fact in the 21st century, as technology, experience, and scientific knowledge grow.

Robotic missions equipped with cameras and sensors already collect information about the solar system and beam it back to earth by radio. The Pathfinder investigations and the discovery of possible ancient life on Mars mean the world's attention is now focused on space once more.

Left *Neil Armstrong climbed down from the Apollo 11 lunar module in July 20, 1969—the first person on the moon.*

Right *Human missions to the moon and Mars may soon become a reality. Space colonies may cease to be science fiction.*

Index

Picture credits

Picture Researcher: Lynda Marshall *Maps:* Mountain High Maps © Digital Wisdom. *Illustrations:* JB Illustrations (Julian Baker); Trevor Bounford; Alastair Campbell; Kevin Jones Associates; Sally Launder; Nicholas Rowland; John Woodcock *Photographs:* Bridgeman Art Library: Private Collection, 4BR; Stapleton Collection, 10B, 13; Museum of Mankind, London; Biblioteca Nazionale Centrale, Florence; Biblioteca Del ICI, Madrid, 15; Christies Images, London, 18; British Museum, London, 21BL; National Library of Australia, Canberra, 22TR; British Library, London, 24TR&26. Corbis; GettyOneStone; Kon Tiki Museum, Oslo, 25BL; Corel Photo Disk; Digital Vision; Aztec New Media Corp.; PhotoDisc; NASA, 30.